BREAKFAST & BRUNCH

CLASSIC RECIPES

Publications International, Ltd.
Favorite Brand Name Recipes at www.fbnr.com

Microwave Cooking: Microwave ovens vary in wattage. Use the cooking times as
guidelines and check for doneness before adding more time.

Preparation/Cooking Times: Preparation times are based on the approximate amount
of time required to assemble the recipe before cooking, baking, chilling or serving. These
times include preparation steps such as measuring, chopping and mixing. The fact that
some preparations and cooking can be done simultaneously is taken into account.
Preparation of optional ingredients and serving suggestions is not included.

Table of Contents

Down-Home Favorites

Weekends are the perfect time to treat yourself to leisurely mornings. So, snuggle up to the table and rediscover some of your most beloved breakfast foods.

Waffles

2 1/4 cups all-purpose flour
2 tablespoons sugar
1 tablespoon baking powder
1/2 teaspoon salt
2 cups milk
2 eggs, beaten
1/4 cup vegetable oil

1. Preheat waffle iron; grease lightly.

2. Sift flour, sugar, baking powder and salt in large bowl. Combine milk, eggs and oil in medium bowl. Stir liquid ingredients into dry ingredients until moistened.

3. For each waffle, pour about 3/4 cup batter onto waffle iron. Close lid and bake until steaming stops.* Garnish as desired.

Makes about 6 round waffles

Check the manufacturer's directions for recommended amount of batter and baking time.

Chocolate Waffles: Substitute 1/4 cup unsweetened cocoa powder for 1/4 cup flour and add 1/4 teaspoon vanilla extract to liquid ingredients. Proceed as directed above.

Three-Egg Omelet

1 tablespoon butter or margarine

3 eggs, lightly beaten

Salt and black pepper

Fillings: Shredded cheese, shredded crabmeat, cooked sliced mushrooms, cooked chopped onion, avocado slices, chopped ham, cooked small shrimp, cooked chopped bell pepper, chopped tomatoes, cooked chopped asparagus and/or cooked chopped broccoli

1. Melt butter in 10-inch skillet over medium heat. Add eggs; lift cooked edges with spatula to allow uncooked eggs to flow under cooked portion. Season with salt and black pepper to taste. Shake pan to loosen omelet. Cook until set.

2. Place desired fillings on ½ of omelet. Fold in half. Transfer to serving plate. Serve immediately.   *Makes 1 serving*

Three-Egg Omelet

Old-Fashioned Cake Doughnuts

3¾ cups all-purpose flour

1 tablespoon baking powder

1 teaspoon ground cinnamon

¾ teaspoon salt

½ teaspoon ground nutmeg

3 eggs

¾ cup granulated sugar

1 cup applesauce

2 tablespoons butter, melted

1 quart vegetable oil

2 cups sifted powdered sugar

3 tablespoons milk

½ teaspoon vanilla

Colored sprinkles (optional)

Combine flour, baking powder, cinnamon, salt and nutmeg in medium bowl. Beat eggs in large bowl with electric mixer at high speed until frothy. Gradually beat in granulated sugar. Continue beating at high speed 4 minutes until thick and lemon colored, scraping down side of bowl once. Reduce speed to low; beat in applesauce and butter.

Beat in flour mixture until well blended. Divide dough into halves. Place each half on large piece of plastic wrap. Pat each half into 5-inch square; wrap in plastic wrap. Refrigerate 3 hours or until well chilled.

Pour oil into large Dutch oven. Place deep-fry thermometer in oil. Heat oil over medium heat until thermometer registers 375°F. Adjust heat as necessary to maintain temperature at 375°F. To prepare glaze, stir together powdered sugar, milk and vanilla in small bowl until smooth. Cover; set aside.

Old-Fashioned Cake Doughnuts

Roll out 1 dough half to ³/₈-inch thickness. Cut dough with floured 3-inch doughnut cutter; repeat with remaining dough. Reserve doughnut holes. Reroll scraps; cut dough again.

Place 4 doughnuts and holes in hot oil. Cook 2 minutes or until golden brown, turning often. Remove with slotted spoon; drain on paper towels. Repeat with remaining doughnuts and holes. Spread glaze over warm doughnuts; decorate with sprinkles, if desired.

Makes 12 doughnuts and holes

11

Baked French Toast Wedges

4 whole BAYS® English muffins, cut into 1-inch cubes

3 large eggs

$^1/_2$ cup sugar

1 teaspoon cinnamon

1 teaspoon vanilla

$^1/_4$ teaspoon salt

1$^2/_3$ cups half-and-half, whipping cream or whole milk

2 tablespoons butter or margarine, melted

$^1/_8$ teaspoon nutmeg, preferably freshly grated

Spray 10-inch quiche dish or deep dish pie plate with non-stick cooking spray. Arrange muffins in a single layer in dish. In a medium bowl, beat together eggs and combined sugar and cinnamon. Stir in vanilla and salt; mix well. Add half-and-half and melted butter or margarine, mixing well. Pour evenly over muffins; press down on muffins to moisten with liquid. Sprinkle nutmeg evenly over mixture. Cover and refrigerate overnight, if desired, or bake immediately.

Bake in 350°F oven for 40 to 45 minutes or until puffed and golden brown. Transfer to cooling rack; cool at least 10 minutes before serving.* Cut into wedges and serve warm with desired fruit topping or heated maple syrup. *Makes 6 servings*

At this point, French toast may be cooled completely, cut into wedges, placed between sheets of waxed paper in a plastic freezer storage bag and frozen up to 1 month. Place wedges on baking sheet and bake in 350°F oven for 8 to 10 minutes or until thawed and heated through.

Mixed Fruit Topping: Combine 1 kiwifruit, peeled and diced, $\frac{1}{2}$ cup fresh raspberries and 1 ripe small banana, sliced with 2 tablespoons honey and 2 teaspoons fresh lime juice. Let stand 5 minutes.

Strawberry Topping: Combine $1\frac{1}{4}$ cups thinly sliced strawberries, $\frac{1}{4}$ cup strawberry jam or currant jelly and 1 teaspoon orange juice** in a microwave safe bowl. Cover and cook at high power 1 minute or until warm. (Or, heat in a small saucepan over medium heat until warm.)

**Almond or orange-flavored liqueur may be substituted, if desired.

Peachy Keen Topping: Combine $\frac{1}{4}$ cup peach or apricot preserves and 1 tablespoon pineapple or apple juice.*** Add 1 peeled and diced ripe peach or 1 cup diced thawed frozen sliced peaches, $\frac{1}{4}$ cup fresh or partially thawed frozen blueberries, mixing well. Serve at room temperature or heat as for Strawberry Topping above.

***Almond or orange-flavored liqueur may be substituted, if desired.

Serve any leftover fruit toppings over a scoop of vanilla ice cream for a quick and delicious fruit-and-cream snack or dessert.

French Toast Strata

4 ounces day-old French or Italian bread, cut into ³/4-inch cubes
  (about 4 cups)

¹/3 cup golden raisins

1 package (3 ounces) cream cheese, cut into ¹/4-inch cubes

3 eggs

1¹/2 cups milk

¹/2 cup maple-flavored pancake syrup

1 teaspoon vanilla

2 tablespoons sugar

1 teaspoon ground cinnamon

Additional maple-flavored pancake syrup (optional)

Spray 11×7-inch baking dish with nonstick cooking spray.

Place bread cubes in even layer in prepared dish; sprinkle raisins and cream cheese evenly over bread.

Beat eggs in medium bowl with electric mixer at medium speed until blended. Add milk, ¹/2 cup pancake syrup and vanilla; mix well. Pour egg mixture evenly over bread mixture. Cover; refrigerate at least 4 hours or overnight.

Preheat oven to 350°F. Combine sugar and cinnamon in small bowl; sprinkle evenly over strata.

Bake, uncovered, 40 to 45 minutes or until puffed, golden brown and knife inserted in center comes out clean. Cut into squares and serve with additional pancake syrup, if desired. *Makes 6 servings*

French Toast Strata

Cheesy Potato Pancakes

1½ quarts prepared instant mashed potatoes, cooked dry and cooled
1½ cups (6 ounces) shredded Wisconsin Colby or Muenster cheese
    4 eggs, lightly beaten
1½ cups all-purpose flour, divided
  ¾ cup chopped fresh parsley
  ⅓ cup chopped fresh chives
1½ teaspoons dried thyme, rosemary or sage leaves
    2 eggs, lightly beaten

1. In large bowl, combine potatoes, cheese, 4 beaten eggs, ¾ cup flour and herbs; mix well. Cover and refrigerate at least 4 hours before molding and preparing.

2. To prepare, form 18 (3-inch) patties. Dip in 2 beaten eggs and dredge in remaining ¾ cup flour. Cook each patty in nonstick skillet over medium heat 3 minutes per side or until crisp, golden brown and heated through.

3. Serve warm with eggs or omelets, or serve with sour cream and sliced pan-fried apples or applesauce. *Makes 4 to 6 servings*

Variation: Substitute Wisconsin Cheddar or Smoked Cheddar for Colby or Muenster.

Favorite recipe from **Wisconsin Milk Marketing Board**

Cheesy Potato Pancakes

Basic Muffins

1 ³/₄ cups all-purpose flour
¹/₃ cup sugar
2 teaspoons baking powder
¹/₂ teaspoon salt
¹/₄ cup cold butter, cut into 4 pieces
¹/₂ cup milk
1 large egg, beaten

1. Heat oven to 400°F. Fit food processor with steel blade. Measure flour, sugar, baking powder and salt into work bowl. Process using on/off pulsing action to mix. Add butter; process using on/off pulsing action 8 to 10 times or until mixture resembles coarse crumbs.

2. Combine milk and egg. Pour over flour mixture. Process on/off 5 or 6 times, or just until flour is moistened. Do not overprocess. Batter should be lumpy.

3. Spoon batter into greased muffin cups, filling each about ²/₃ full. Bake until golden, 20 to 25 minutes. Serve warm.   *Makes 1 dozen muffins*

Blueberry Muffins: Prepare batter as directed for Basic Muffins, increasing sugar to ¹/₂ cup. Gently fold 1 cup fresh or thawed frozen blueberries or ³/₄ cup well drained canned blueberries into batter just before spooning into muffin cups. Bake as directed for Basic Muffins.

Date or Raisin Muffins: Prepare batter as directed for Basic Muffins, adding 1 cup chopped, pitted dates or dark raisins to flour mixture before adding milk and egg. Process on/off, then add milk and egg. Continue as directed for Basic Muffins.

Lemon Nut Muffins: Prepare batter as directed for Basic Muffins, adding 1 cup chopped nuts and 2 teaspoons grated lemon peel to flour mixture before adding milk and egg. Process on/off, then add milk and egg. Continue as directed for Basic Muffins.

Cinnamon Surprise Muffins: Prepare batter as directed for Basic Muffins, adding $1/4$ teaspoon ground cinnamon to work bowl with flour, sugar, baking powder and salt. Fill muffin cups $1/2$ full of batter, then drop 1 teaspoon fruit jelly, jam or preserves in center of batter in each cup. Cover with remaining batter. Bake as directed for Basic Muffins.

Cranberry Muffins: Prepare batter as directed for Basic Muffins, increasing sugar to $1/2$ cup. Gently fold 1 cup chopped fresh cranberries into batter just before spooning into muffin cups. Bake as directed for Basic Muffins.

PB & J French Toast

¼ cup preserves, any flavor

6 slices whole wheat bread, divided

¼ cup creamy peanut butter

½ cup egg substitute

¼ cup skim milk

2 tablespoons margarine or butter

1 large banana, sliced

1 tablespoon honey

1 tablespoon orange juice

1 tablespoon PLANTERS® Dry Roasted Unsalted Peanuts, chopped

Low fat vanilla yogurt, optional

1. Spread preserves evenly over 3 bread slices. Spread peanut butter evenly over remaining bread slices. Press preserves and peanut butter slices together to form 3 sandwiches; cut each diagonally in half.

2. Combine egg substitute and milk in shallow bowl. Dip each sandwich in egg mixture to coat.

3. Cook sandwiches in margarine or butter in large nonstick griddle or skillet over medium-high heat for 2 minutes on each side or until golden. Keep warm.

4. Mix banana slices, honey, orange juice and peanuts in small bowl. Arrange sandwiches on platter; top with banana mixture. Serve warm with a dollop of yogurt if desired.   *Makes 6 servings*

Prep Time: 25 minutes
Cook Time: 10 minutes

PB & J French Toast

Biscuits 'n Gravy

BISCUITS

     WESSON® No-Stick Cooking Spray

  2 cups self-rising flour

  2 teaspoons sugar

1 $^1/_2$ teaspoons baking powder

  $^3/_4$ cup buttermilk

  $^1/_4$ cup WESSON® Vegetable Oil

GRAVY

  1 pound bulk pork sausage

  $^1/_4$ cup all-purpose flour

  2 cups milk

  $^1/_4$ teaspoon salt

  $^1/_4$ teaspoon pepper

Biscuits

Preheat oven to 450°F. Lightly spray a baking sheet with Wesson®
Cooking Spray. In a large bowl, combine flour, sugar and baking powder;
blend well. In a small bowl, whisk together buttermilk and Wesson® Oil;
add to dry ingredients and mix until dough is moist but not sticky. On a
lightly floured surface, knead dough lightly 4 or 5 times. Roll dough to a
$^3/_4$-inch thickness; cut with a 4-inch biscuit cutter. Knead any scraps
together and repeat cutting method. Place biscuits on baking sheet and
bake 10 to 15 minutes or until lightly browned. Keep warm.

Gravy

Meanwhile, in a large skillet, cook and crumble sausage until brown. Reserve 1/4 cup of drippings in skillet; drain sausage well. Set aside. Add flour to drippings in skillet; stir until smooth. Cook over medium heat for 2 to 3 minutes or until dark brown, stirring constantly. Gradually add milk, stirring constantly until smooth and thickened. (Use more milk if necessary to achieve desired consistency.) Stir in salt, pepper and sausage; heat through. Serve over hot split biscuits.

Makes 6 servings (2 biscuits each)

Hash Brown Bake

1 packet (1 ounce) HIDDEN VALLEY® Original Ranch® Dressing Mix

1 1/4 cups milk

3 ounces cream cheese

6 cups hash browns, frozen shredded potatoes

1 tablespoon bacon bits

1/2 cup shredded Sharp Cheddar cheese

In blender, combine dressing mix, milk and cream cheese. Pour over potatoes and bacon bits in 9-inch baking dish. Top with cheese. Bake at 350°F for 35 minutes.

Makes 4 servings

Sunrise French Toast

2 cups cholesterol-free egg substitute

$1/2$ cup evaporated skimmed milk

1 teaspoon grated orange peel

1 teaspoon vanilla

$1/4$ teaspoon ground cinnamon

1 loaf (1 pound) Italian bread, cut into $1/2$-inch-thick slices (about 20 slices)

1 jar (10 ounces) no-sugar-added orange marmalade

Nonstick cooking spray

Powdered sugar

Maple-flavored syrup (optional)

1. Preheat oven to 400°F. Combine egg substitute, milk, orange peel, vanilla and cinnamon in medium bowl. Set aside.

2. Spread 1 bread slice with 1 tablespoon marmalade to within $1/2$ inch of edge. Top with another bread slice. Repeat with remaining bread and marmalade.

3. Spray griddle or large skillet with cooking spray; heat over medium heat until hot. Dip sandwiches in egg substitute mixture. Do not soak. Cook sandwiches in batches 2 to 3 minutes on each side or until golden brown.

4. Transfer toasted sandwiches to 15×10-inch jelly-roll pan. Bake 10 to 12 minutes or until sides are sealed. Dust with powdered sugar and serve with syrup. *Makes 5 servings*

Sunrise French Toast

Buttermilk Pancakes

2 cups all-purpose flour

1 tablespoon sugar

1 1/2 teaspoons baking powder

1/2 teaspoon baking soda

1/2 teaspoon salt

1 egg, beaten

1 1/2 cups buttermilk

1/4 cup vegetable oil

1. Sift flour, sugar, baking powder, baking soda and salt into large bowl.

2. Combine egg, buttermilk and oil in medium bowl. Stir liquid ingredients into dry ingredients until moistened.

3. Preheat griddle or large skillet over medium heat; grease lightly. Pour about 1/2 cup batter onto hot griddle for each pancake. Cook until tops of pancakes are bubbly and appear dry; turn and cook until browned, about 2 minutes. *Makes about 12 (5-inch) pancakes*

Silver Dollar Pancakes: Use 1 tablespoon batter for each pancake. Cook as directed above.

Corned Beef Hash

6 to 7 medium red boiling potatoes, peeled

1 teaspoon salt, divided

3 tablespoons parve margarine

1 cup chopped onion

$^{1}/_{3}$ cup chopped seeded red bell pepper

$^{1}/_{4}$ teaspoon freshly ground black pepper

2 cups chopped cooked HEBREW NATIONAL® Corned Beef

Place potatoes in medium saucepan; cover with water. Cover; bring to a boil over high heat. Add $^{1}/_{4}$ teaspoon salt. Boil 12 to 15 minutes or until fork-tender. Drain; rinse with cold water. Cut potatoes into $^{1}/_{2}$-inch pieces.

Melt margarine in large nonstick skillet over medium heat. Add onion and bell pepper; cook and stir 5 minutes. Add potatoes, remaining $^{3}/_{4}$ teaspoon salt and black pepper; cook, stirring occasionally, 15 minutes or until browned. Stir corned beef into potato mixture. Cook 3 minutes or until heated through. *Makes 4 servings*

Red potatoes work best in this recipe because they have a waxy texture. This helps them retain their shape and not become mushy after being cooked.

Encore Eggs Benedict

Hollandaise Sauce (recipe follows)
8 eggs
16 slices Canadian bacon
4 English muffins, split, toasted and buttered

1. Prepare Hollandaise Sauce.

2. Bring 2 to 3 inches water to a boil in medium saucepan over medium-high heat. Reduce heat to a simmer. Break 1 egg into small dish. Holding dish close to surface of simmering water, carefully slip egg into water. Repeat with 1 egg. Cook 3 to 5 minutes or until yolks are just set. Remove eggs and drain on paper towels. Repeat with remaining eggs.

3. Cook bacon in large skillet over medium-low heat, turning occasionally.

4. Top each English muffin half with 2 slices bacon, 1 poached egg and 1 tablespoon Hollandaise Sauce. Serve immediately.

Makes 4 servings

Hollandaise Sauce

3 egg yolks
1 tablespoon lemon juice
1 teaspoon dry mustard
1/4 teaspoon salt
Dash ground red pepper (optional)
1/2 cup (1 stick) butter, cut into eighths

Encore Eggs Benedict

1. Beat together egg yolks, lemon juice, mustard, salt and pepper in small saucepan until blended. Add $^1/_4$ cup butter.

2. Cook over low heat, stirring with wire whisk until butter is melted. Slowly add remaining $^1/_4$ cup butter; whisk constantly until butter is melted and sauce is thickened. *Makes $^3/_4$ cup*

Variation: Substitute smoked salmon for Canadian bacon. Use approximately 2 ounces smoked salmon per serving.

Country-Fresh Eggs

*Who says eggs have to be boring? Add
excitement to your morning with one
of the delectable recipes in this chapter.
Make room at the table because the
whole family will enjoy waking up to
these satisfying egg dishes.*

Breakfast Pizza

1 can (10 ounces) refrigerated pizza dough
1 package (7 ounces) pre-browned fully cooked sausage patties,
    thawed
3 eggs
1/2 cup milk
1 teaspoon dried Italian seasoning
2 cups (8 ounces) shredded pizza-style cheese

1. Preheat oven to 425°F. For crust, unroll pizza dough and pat onto bottom and up side of greased 12-inch pizza pan. Bake 5 minutes or until set, but not browned.

2. While crust is baking, cut sausages into 1/2-inch pieces. Whisk together eggs, milk and Italian seasoning in medium bowl until well blended. Season to taste with salt and black pepper.

3. Spoon sausages over crust; sprinkle with cheese. Carefully pour egg mixture over sausage and cheese. Bake 15 to 20 minutes or until eggs are set and crust is golden. *Makes 6 servings*

Baked Eggs Florentine

2 packages (10 ounces each) frozen creamed spinach
4 slices (1/8 inch thick) deli ham, about 5 to 6 ounces
4 eggs
   Salt and black pepper
1/8 teaspoon ground nutmeg
1/2 cup (2 ounces) shredded provolone cheese
2 tablespoons chopped roasted red pepper

1. Preheat oven to 450°F. Make small cut in each package of spinach. Microwave at HIGH 5 to 6 minutes, turning packages halfway through cooking time.

2. Meanwhile, grease 8-inch square baking pan. Place ham slices on bottom of prepared pan, overlapping slightly. Spread spinach mixture over ham slices.

3. Make 4 indentations in spinach. Carefully break 1 egg in each. Season to taste with salt and black pepper. Sprinkle with nutmeg.

4. Bake 16 to 19 minutes or until eggs are set. Remove from oven. Sprinkle cheese and red pepper over top. Return to oven and bake 1 to 2 minutes longer or until cheese is melted. Serve immediately.

Makes 4 servings

Prep & Cook Time: 28 minutes

Serving Suggestion: Serve with toasted English muffin halves and fresh pineapple pieces.

Baked Egg Florentine

Easy Morning Strata

1 pound BOB EVANS® Original Recipe Roll Sausage

8 eggs

10 slices bread, cut into cubes (about 10 cups)

3 cups milk

2 cups (8 ounces) shredded Cheddar cheese

2 cups (8 ounces) sliced fresh mushrooms

1 (10-ounce) package frozen cut asparagus, thawed and drained

2 tablespoons butter or margarine, melted

2 tablespoons all-purpose flour

1 tablespoon dry mustard

2 teaspoons dried basil leaves

1 teaspoon salt

Crumble sausage into large skillet. Cook over medium heat until browned, stirring occasionally. Drain off any drippings. Whisk eggs in large bowl. Add sausage and remaining ingredients; mix well. Spoon into greased 13×9-inch baking dish. Cover; refrigerate 8 hours or overnight. Preheat oven to 350°F. Bake 60 to 70 minutes or until knife inserted near center comes out clean. Let stand 5 minutes before cutting into squares; serve hot. Refrigerate leftovers. *Makes 10 to 12 servings*

Easy Morning Strata

Southwest Ham 'n Cheese Quiche

    4 (8-inch) flour tortillas
    2 tablespoons butter or margarine, melted
    2 cups pizza 4-cheese blend
 1^1/$_2$ cups (8 ounces) diced CURE 81® ham
   ^{1}/$_2$ cup sour cream
   ^{1}/$_4$ cup salsa
    3 eggs, beaten
      Salsa
      Sour cream

Heat oven to 350°F. Cut 3 tortillas in half. Place remaining whole tortilla in bottom of greased 10-inch quiche dish or tart pan; brush with melted butter. Arrange tortilla halves around edge of dish, rounded sides up, overlapping to form pastry shell. Brush with remaining butter. Place 9-inch round cake pan inside quiche dish. Bake 5 minutes. Cool; remove cake pan. In bowl, combine cheese and ham. Stir in sour cream, salsa and eggs. Pour into tortilla shell. Bake 55 to 60 minutes or until knife inserted in center comes out clean. Let stand 5 minutes. Serve with additional salsa and sour cream.   *Makes 6 servings*

*Cut some of the fat from this quiche by using a lower
fat cheese blend and nonfat sour cream. It will still
have all the flavor without all the fat.*

Southwest Ham 'n Cheese Quiche

Egg Blossoms

4 sheets phyllo pastry

2 tablespoons butter, melted

4 teaspoons grated Parmesan cheese

4 large eggs

4 teaspoons minced green onion

Salt and black pepper

Tomato Sauce (recipe follows, optional)

1. Prepare Tomato Sauce, if desired; set aside. Preheat oven to 350°F. Grease 4 (2½-inch) muffin cups. Brush 1 sheet of phyllo with butter. Top with another sheet; brush with butter. Cut stack into 6 (4-inch) squares. Repeat with remaining 2 sheets. Stack 3 squares together, rotating so corners do not overlap. Press into prepared muffin cup. Repeat with remaining squares.

2. Sprinkle 1 teaspoon cheese into each phyllo-lined cup. Break 1 egg into each cup. Sprinkle onion over eggs. Season with salt and pepper. Bake 15 to 20 minutes or until pastry is golden and eggs are set. Serve with Tomato Sauce, if desired.   *Makes 4 servings*

Tomato Sauce

1 can (16 ounces) whole tomatoes, undrained and chopped

1 clove garlic, minced

½ cup chopped onion

1 tablespoon white wine vinegar

½ teaspoon salt

¼ teaspoon dried oregano leaves

Combine all ingredients in medium saucepan. Cook and stir over medium heat until onion is tender, about 20 minutes. Serve warm.

Egg Blossom

Breakfast Wraps

1 (16-ounce) can ROSARITA® Vegetarian Refried Beans
1 cup salsa
3 (4-ounce) containers fat free egg substitute (or 12 eggs)
2 tablespoons water
$^1/_4$ teaspoon garlic powder
$^1/_4$ teaspoon onion powder
$^1/_8$ teaspoon black pepper
   WESSON® No-Stick Cooking Spray
8 fat free burrito-size flour tortillas, warmed
$^1/_4$ cup *each:* no-fat shredded Cheddar and Monterey Jack Cheeses,
   blended

1. Preheat oven to 350°F.

2. In medium saucepan, over low heat, heat Rosarita Refried Beans and salsa until hot.

3. Meanwhile, in medium bowl, combine egg substitute, water, garlic powder, onion powder and pepper; beat well.

4. In large non-stick skillet, sprayed with Wesson Cooking Spray, scramble and cook egg mixture until fluffy and firm; remove from heat.

5. Spread about $^1/_3$ *cup* bean mixture over each tortilla; top with $^1/_4$ *cup* egg mixture; sprinkle with *1 tablespoon* cheeses.

6. Roll tortillas burrito style.

7. Bake, covered, on cookie sheet sprayed with Wesson Cooking Spray, for 20 minutes. Serve.   *Makes 8 (7-ounce) servings*

Cherry Brunch Pie

¹/2 pound bulk pork sausage

1 (16-ounce) can tart cherries, drained and coarsely chopped

1 cup shredded sharp Cheddar cheese (about 4 ounces)

1 cup buttermilk baking mix

1 teaspoon dried basil

¹/2 teaspoon salt, or to taste

¹/8 teaspoon ground black pepper, or to taste

4 eggs, lightly beaten

1 ¹/2 cups milk

Cook sausage in large skillet until brown, breaking it into small pieces as it cooks; drain off fat. Remove from heat. Add cherries; mix well. Spoon sausage mixture into 10-inch deep-dish pie plate. Top with cheese.

Combine baking mix, basil, salt and pepper in medium mixing bowl; mix well. Add eggs and milk; beat until smooth. Spread over cheese.

Bake in preheated 400°F oven 35 to 40 minutes or until knife inserted in center comes out clean. Let cool 5 minutes. Cut into wedges. Serve immediately.   *Makes 6 servings*

Note: If desired, 1 ¹/2 cups frozen unsweetened tart cherries can be substituted for canned cherries. Partly thaw cherries, then coarsely chop them before adding to sausage.

Favorite recipe from **Cherry Marketing Institute**

Sausage Vegetable Frittata

5 eggs

$^1/_4$ cup milk

2 tablespoons grated Parmesan cheese

$^1/_2$ teaspoon dried oregano leaves

$^1/_2$ teaspoon black pepper

1 (10-ounce) package BOB EVANS® Skinless Link Sausage

2 tablespoons butter or margarine

1 small zucchini, sliced (about 1 cup)

$^1/_2$ cup shredded carrots

$^1/_3$ cup sliced green onions with tops

$^3/_4$ cup (3 ounces) shredded Swiss cheese

Carrot curls (optional)

Whisk eggs in medium bowl; stir in milk, Parmesan cheese, oregano and pepper. Set aside. Cook sausage in large skillet over medium heat until browned, turning occasionally. Drain off any drippings. Remove sausage from skillet and cut into $^1/_2$-inch lengths. Melt butter in same skillet. Add zucchini, shredded carrots and onions; cook and stir over medium heat until tender. Top with sausage, then Swiss cheese. Pour egg mixture over vegetable mixture. Stir gently to combine. Cook, without stirring, over low heat 8 to 10 minutes or until center is almost set. Remove from heat. Let stand 5 minutes before cutting into wedges; serve hot. Garnish with carrot curls, if desired. Refrigerate leftovers.   *Makes 4 to 6 servings*

Sausage Vegetable Frittata

Crunchy Ranch-Style Eggs

2 cans (10 ounces each) tomatoes and green chilies, drained

1 1/3 cups *French's® Taste Toppers™ French Fried Onions, divided*

2 tablespoons *Frank's® RedHot® Sauce*

2 tablespoons *French's® Worcestershire Sauce*

6 eggs

1 cup (4 ounces) shredded Cheddar cheese

Preheat oven to 400°F. Grease 2-quart shallow baking dish. Combine tomatoes, *2/3 cup* **Taste Toppers**, **RedHot** Sauce and Worcestershire in prepared dish. Make 6 indentations in mixture. Break 1 egg into each indentation.

Bake, uncovered, 15 to 20 minutes or until eggs are set. Top with cheese and remaining *2/3 cup* **Taste Toppers**. Bake 1 minute or until **Taste Toppers** are golden. *Makes 6 servings*

Prep Time: 5 minutes
Cook Time: 16 minutes

Tip: Recipe may be prepared in individual ramekin dishes. Bake until eggs are set.

Crunchy Ranch-Style Egg

Spinach Sensation

$^1/_2$ pound bacon slices

1 cup (8 ounces) sour cream

3 eggs, separated

2 tablespoons all-purpose flour

$^1/_8$ teaspoon black pepper

1 package (10 ounces) frozen chopped spinach, thawed and
   squeezed dry

$^1/_2$ cup (2 ounces) shredded sharp Cheddar cheese

$^1/_2$ cup dry bread crumbs

1 tablespoon margarine or butter, melted

Preheat oven to 350°F. Spray 2-quart round baking dish with nonstick cooking spray.

Place bacon in single layer in large skillet; cook over medium heat until crisp. Remove from skillet; drain on paper towels. Crumble and set aside.

Combine sour cream, egg yolks, flour and pepper in large bowl; set aside. Beat egg whites in medium bowl with electric mixer at high speed until stiff peaks form. Stir $^1/_4$ of egg whites into sour cream mixture; fold in remaining egg whites.

Arrange half of spinach in prepared dish. Top with half of sour cream mixture. Sprinkle $^1/_4$ cup cheese over sour cream mixture. Sprinkle bacon over cheese. Repeat layers, ending with remaining $^1/_4$ cup cheese.

Combine bread crumbs and margarine in small bowl; sprinkle evenly over cheese.

Bake, uncovered, 30 to 35 minutes or until egg mixture is set. Let stand 5 minutes before serving.   *Makes 6 servings*

Spinach Sensation

Potato Breakfast Custard

3 large Colorado russet variety potatoes, peeled and thinly sliced
    Salt and black pepper
8 ounces low-fat bulk sausage, cooked and crumbled*
1/3 cup roasted red pepper, thinly sliced or 1 jar (2 ounces) sliced
    pimientos, drained
3 eggs
1 cup low-fat milk
3 tablespoons chopped chives or green onion tops
3/4 teaspoon dried thyme or oregano leaves, crushed
    Salsa and sour cream (optional)

Substitute 6 ounces finely diced lean ham or 6 ounces crumbled, cooked turkey bacon for sausage, if desired.

Preheat oven to 375°F. Butter 8- or 9-inch square baking dish or other small casserole. Arrange 1/2 of potatoes in baking dish. Season to taste with salt and black pepper. Cover with 1/2 of sausage. Arrange remaining potatoes over sausage; season to taste with salt and black pepper. Top with remaining sausage and red peppers. Beat eggs, milk, chives and thyme until blended. Pour over potatoes. Cover baking dish with foil and bake 45 to 50 minutes or until potatoes are tender. Uncover and bake 5 to 10 minutes longer. Serve with salsa and sour cream, if desired.

Makes 4 to 5 servings

Favorite recipe from **Colorado Potato Administrative Committee**

BUSINESS REPLY MAIL

FIRST-CLASS MAIL PERMIT NO. 24 MT. MORRIS, IL

POSTAGE WILL BE PAID BY ADDRESSEE

EASY HOME COOKING
PO BOX 520
MT MORRIS IL 61054-7451

Puffy Orange Omelets

5 eggs, separated
2 tablespoons all-purpose flour
1 tablespoon grated orange peel
4 tablespoons sugar, divided
$^3/_4$ cup orange juice
2 tablespoons butter or margarine
2 tablespoons brown sugar

1. Preheat oven to 375°F. Whisk together egg yolks, flour and orange peel in large bowl until well blended.

2. Combine egg whites and 2 tablespoons sugar in medium bowl. Beat egg white mixture on high speed of electric mixer 3 to 5 minutes or until stiff, but not dry, peaks form. Fold into egg yolk mixture; set aside.

3. Combine orange juice, butter and brown sugar in small saucepan. Cook and stir over medium heat 3 to 5 minutes or until butter melts and sauce is heated through.

4. Grease 6 (5-ounce) soufflé dishes or custard cups; lightly sprinkle with remaining 2 tablespoons sugar, shaking out excess. Place 1 tablespoon orange sauce in bottom of each soufflé dish, reserving remaining sauce. Spoon egg mixture equally into dishes.

5. Place soufflé dishes in shallow baking pan. Bake 15 to 20 minutes or until tops are golden brown. Serve immediately with reserved warm orange sauce.   *Makes 6 servings*

Rise 'n' Shine Breads

Nothing gets the gang out of bed faster than the wonderful aroma of fresh-baked bread coming from the kitchen. And with these fabulous breads, muffins and coffeecakes, waiting in line at the bakery will be a thing of the past.

Cherry Orange Poppy Seed Muffins

2 cups all-purpose flour

$^3/_4$ cup granulated sugar

1 tablespoon baking powder

1 tablespoon poppy seeds

$^1/_4$ teaspoon salt

1 cup milk

$^1/_4$ cup ($^1/_2$ stick) butter, melted

1 egg, slightly beaten

$^1/_2$ cup dried tart cherries

3 tablespoons grated orange peel

Combine flour, sugar, baking powder, poppy seeds and salt in large mixing bowl. Add milk, melted butter and egg, stirring just until dry ingredients are moistened. Gently stir in cherries and orange peel. Fill paper-lined muffin cups $^3/_4$ full.

Bake in preheated 400°F oven 18 to 22 minutes or until wooden pick inserted in center comes out clean. Let cool in pan 5 minutes. Remove from pan and serve warm or let cool completely.   *Makes 12 muffins*

Favorite recipe from **Cherry Marketing Institute**

Chocolate Popovers

$^3/_4$ cup plus 2 tablespoons all-purpose flour

$^1/_4$ cup granulated sugar

2 tablespoons unsweetened cocoa powder

$^1/_4$ teaspoon salt

4 eggs

1 cup milk

2 tablespoons butter, melted

$^1/_2$ teaspoon vanilla

Powdered sugar

Position rack in lower third of oven. Preheat oven to 375°F. Grease 6-cup popover pan or 6 (6-ounce) custard cups. Set custard cups in jelly-roll pan for easier handling.

Sift flour, granulated sugar, cocoa and salt into medium bowl; set aside. Beat eggs in large bowl with electric mixer at low speed 1 minute. Beat in milk, butter and vanilla. Beat in flour mixture until smooth. Pour batter into prepared pan. Bake 50 minutes.

Place pieces of waxed paper under wire rack to keep counter clean. Immediately remove popovers to wire rack. Place powdered sugar in fine-mesh sieve. Generously sprinkle powdered sugar over popovers. Serve immediately. *Makes 6 popovers*

Chocolate Popovers

Honey-Mustard Scones

3¹/₂ to 3³/₄ cups all-purpose flour

   5 teaspoons DAVIS® Baking Powder

   1 teaspoon salt

³/₄ cup margarine

   3 eggs

¹/₂ cup milk

¹/₃ cup GREY POUPON® COUNTRY DIJON Mustard

¹/₄ cup honey

¹/₂ teaspoon A.1.® Steak Sauce

³/₄ cup finely chopped ham

1. Mix 3¹/₂ cups flour, baking powder and salt in large bowl. With pastry blender, cut in margarine until mixture resembles coarse crumbs; set aside.

2. Beat 2 eggs, milk, mustard, honey and steak sauce in small bowl with wire whisk; add ham. Stir into flour mixture just until blended, adding extra flour if necessary to make soft dough.

3. Roll dough on lightly floured surface into 12×8-inch rectangle. Cut dough into eight 4×3-inch rectangles; cut each rectangle into 2 triangles. Place on greased baking sheets, about 2 inches apart. Beat remaining egg; brush tops of scones with egg.

4. Bake at 425°F for 10 minutes or until golden brown.

Makes 16 scones

Honey-Mustard Scones

Apple Cheddar Scones

1 1/2 cups unsifted all-purpose flour
1/2 cup toasted wheat germ
3 tablespoons sugar
2 teaspoons baking powder
1/2 teaspoon salt
2 tablespoons butter
1 small Washington Rome apple, cored and chopped
1/4 cup shredded Cheddar cheese
1 large egg white
1/2 cup low fat (1%) milk

1. Heat oven to 400°F. Grease an 8-inch round cake pan. In medium-size bowl, combine flour, wheat germ, sugar, baking powder and salt. With two knives or pastry blender, cut in butter until the size of coarse crumbs. Toss chopped apple and cheese in flour mixture.

2. Beat together egg white and milk until well combined. Add to flour mixture, mixing with fork until dough forms. Turn dough out onto lightly floured surface and knead 6 times.

3. Spread dough evenly in cake pan and score deeply with knife into 6 wedges. Bake 25 to 30 minutes or until top springs back when gently pressed. Let stand 5 minutes; remove from pan. Cool before serving.

Makes 6 scones

Favorite recipe from **Washington Apple Commission**

Blueberry Coffee Cake

COFFEE CAKE

$1^{1}/_{2}$ cups all-purpose flour

$^{1}/_{4}$ cup sugar

$2^{1}/_{2}$ teaspoons baking powder

$^{1}/_{2}$ teaspoon salt

$^{1}/_{4}$ teaspoon ground allspice

$^{1}/_{3}$ cup butter or margarine, melted

1 egg

$^{2}/_{3}$ cup milk

$^{3}/_{4}$ cup SMUCKER'S® Blueberry Preserves

TOPPING

$^{1}/_{4}$ cup firmly packed brown sugar

$^{1}/_{4}$ cup chopped walnuts

2 tablespoons flour

1 tablespoon butter or margarine

Grease and flour 8- or 9-inch square baking pan. Lightly spoon flour into measuring cup; level off. In medium bowl, combine $1^{1}/_{2}$ cups flour, sugar, baking powder, salt and allspice. Add melted butter, egg and milk. Mix vigorously until well blended.

Pour half of batter into greased and floured pan; spread preserves evenly over batter. Top with remaining batter.

Combine topping ingredients; mix until crumbly. Sprinkle over top of coffee cake.

Bake at 400°F for 20 to 25 minutes or until toothpick inserted in center comes out clean.   *Makes 9 servings*

Cranberry Oat Bran Muffins

2 cups flour
1 cup oat bran
$^1/_2$ cup packed brown sugar
2 teaspoons baking powder
$^1/_2$ teaspoon baking soda
$^1/_2$ teaspoon salt (optional)
$^1/_2$ cup MIRACLE WHIP® Light
3 egg whites, slightly beaten
$^1/_2$ cup skim milk
$^1/_3$ cup orange juice
1 teaspoon grated orange peel
1 cup coarsely chopped cranberries

• Line 12 medium muffin cups with paper baking cups or spray with nonstick cooking spray.

• Mix together dry ingredients.

• Combine dressing, egg whites, milk, juice and peel.

• Add to dry ingredients just until moistened. Fold in cranberries. Fill prepared muffin cups almost full.

• Bake at 375°F for 15 to 17 minutes or until golden brown.

Makes 12 muffins

Cranberry Oat Bran Muffins

Cheese-Filled Almond Braids

1 recipe Sweet Yeast Dough (page 62)
2 packages (8 ounces each) cream cheese, softened
2/3 cup granulated sugar plus additional
2 eggs, separated
2 tablespoons all-purpose flour
1 1/2 teaspoons almond extract
1 tablespoon water
1/4 cup sliced almonds
Powdered sugar (optional)

1. Prepare Sweet Yeast Dough; let rise as directed. Grease 2 large baking sheets. Combine cream cheese, 2/3 cup granulated sugar, egg yolks, flour and almond extract in large bowl. Beat until smooth.

2. Cut dough in half. Roll out one half into 12×9-inch rectangle on lightly floured surface. Transfer dough to prepared baking sheet.

3. Score dough lengthwise into 3 (3-inch-wide) sections, taking care not to cut completely through dough. Spread half of cream cheese mixture on center section between score marks. Cut dough on outer sections into 1-inch diagonal strips, cutting to within 1/2 inch of filling.

4. Starting at 1 end, fold strips over filling, alternating from left and right, overlapping strips in center to create a braided pattern. Repeat with remaining dough and cream cheese mixture. Cover braids with towels; let rise in warm place about 45 minutes or until doubled in bulk.

5. Preheat oven to 350°F. Mix reserved egg whites with 1 tablespoon water in bowl. Brush braids with egg white mixture. Sprinkle almonds over braids. Sprinkle additional granulated sugar over almonds, if desired.

continued on page 62

Cheese-Filled Almond Braid

Cheese-Filled Almond Braids, continued

6. Bake 25 to 30 minutes or until braids are golden brown and sound hollow when tapped, rotating baking sheets from top to bottom racks halfway through baking. Immediately remove from baking sheets; cool completely on wire racks. Dust with powdered sugar, if desired.

Makes 24 servings (2 coffee cakes)

Sweet Yeast Dough

> 4 to 4$^{1}/_{4}$ cups all-purpose flour, divided
> $^{1}/_{2}$ cup sugar
> 2 packages active dry yeast
> 1 teaspoon salt
> $^{3}/_{4}$ cup milk
> $^{1}/_{4}$ cup butter
> 2 eggs
> 1 teaspoon vanilla

1. Mix 1 cup flour, sugar, yeast and salt in bowl. Heat milk and butter in saucepan over low heat until mixture is 120° to 130°F. (Butter does not need to completely melt.) Beat milk mixture into flour mixture 2 minutes. Beat in eggs, vanilla and 1 cup flour; beat 2 minutes. Stir in enough additional flour, about 2 cups, to make soft dough.

2. Turn out dough onto lightly floured surface; flatten slightly. Knead dough 5 minutes or until smooth and elastic, adding remaining $^{1}/_{4}$ cup flour to prevent sticking if necessary. Shape dough into a ball; place in large greased bowl. Turn dough over so that top is greased. Cover with towel; let rise in warm place 1$^{1}/_{2}$ to 2 hours or until doubled in bulk.

3. Punch down dough. Knead dough on lightly floured surface 1 minute. Cover with towel; let rest 10 minutes.

Calico Spice Muffins

WESSON® No-Stick Cooking Spray

2 cups all-purpose flour

3/4 cup packed brown sugar

2 1/2 teaspoons baking soda

2 teaspoons ground cinnamon

1/2 teaspoon salt

1/2 teaspoon nutmeg

1/2 teaspoon allspice

1/2 cup WESSON® Vegetable or Canola Oil

1/2 cup milk

3 eggs, beaten

2 teaspoons vanilla

2 cups grated carrots

2 cups peeled, cored and diced apples (Pippin, Granny Smith or Rome Beauty)

2/3 cup toasted coconut

2/3 cup toasted sliced almonds

2/3 cup raisins

Preheat oven to 375°F. Spray muffin cups with Wesson® Cooking Spray. In a large bowl, combine *next* 7 ingredients, ending with allspice. In another bowl, stir together Wesson® Oil, milk, eggs and vanilla; mix well. Gradually stir egg mixture into flour mixture until moistened. Fold in the *remaining* ingredients. Fill muffin cups to rim. Bake for 25 minutes or until wooden pick inserted into center comes out clean. Cool 5 minutes. Remove muffins to wire racks. Serve muffins warm or cool.

Makes 1 1/2 dozen muffins

Baked Banana Doughnuts

2 ripe bananas, mashed

2 egg whites

1 tablespoon vegetable oil

1 cup packed brown sugar

1 1/2 cups all-purpose flour

3/4 cup whole wheat flour

2 teaspoons baking powder

1/2 teaspoon baking soda

1/4 teaspoon pumpkin pie spice

1 tablespoon granulated sugar

2 tablespoons chopped walnuts (optional)

Preheat oven to 425°F. Spray baking sheet with nonstick cooking spray. Beat bananas, egg whites, oil and brown sugar in large bowl or food processor. Add flours, baking powder, baking soda and pumpkin pie spice. Mix until well blended. Let stand for five minutes for dough to rise. Scoop out heaping tablespoonfuls of dough onto prepared baking sheet. Using thin rubber spatula or butter knife round out doughnut hole in center of dough (if dough sticks to knife or spatula spray with cooking spray). With spatula, smooth outside edges of dough into round doughnut shape. Repeat until all dough is used. Sprinkle with granulated sugar and walnuts, if desired. Bake 6 to 10 minutes or until tops are golden.

Makes about 22 doughnuts

Variation: Use 8 ounces solid pack pumpkin instead of bananas to make pumpkin doughnuts.

Favorite recipe from **The Sugar Association, Inc.**

Baked Banana Doughnuts

Nutty Cinnamon Sticky Buns

$^1/_3$ **cup margarine or butter**
$^1/_2$ **cup packed brown sugar**
$^1/_2$ **cup PLANTERS® Pecans, chopped**
1 **teaspoon ground cinnamon**
1 **(17.3-ounce) package refrigerated biscuits (8 large biscuits)**

1. Melt margarine or butter in 9-inch round baking pan in 350°F oven.

2. Mix brown sugar, pecans and cinnamon in small bowl; sprinkle over melted margarine or butter in pan. Arrange biscuits in pan with sides touching (biscuits will fit tightly in pan).

3. Bake at 350°F for 25 to 30 minutes or until biscuits are golden brown and center biscuit is fully cooked. Invert pan immediately onto serving plate. Spread any remaining topping from pan on buns. Serve warm.

Makes 8 buns

Preparation Time: 10 minutes
Cook Time: 25 minutes
Total Time: 35 minutes

Chop nuts easily in your food processor using an on/off pulsing action, being careful to process the nuts just until they are chopped.

Nutty Cinnamon Sticky Buns

Blueberry Crumb Cakes

1 8-ounce package cream cheese, softened

1/4 cup sugar

1 egg

1 teaspoon vanilla extract

3 BAYS® English Muffins, lightly toasted

1 cup frozen blueberries, thawed*

   Crumb Topping (recipe follows)

Fresh blueberries may be substituted.

In medium bowl, beat cream cheese, sugar, egg and vanilla until smooth. Spread about 2 rounded tablespoons of cream cheese mixture on each muffin half. Evenly arrange blueberries on top of cream cheese. Sprinkle about 2 tablespoons crumb topping over each muffin. Place muffins on a cookie sheet; bake 20 to 25 minutes in preheated oven at 350°F. Cool 30 minutes before serving.   *Makes 6 servings*

Crumb Topping

2 tablespoons butter or margarine

2 tablespoons flour

1/4 cup packed brown sugar

1/4 cup quick-cooking oats

In a small bowl, with pastry blender, cut butter into flour until mixture resembles coarse crumbs. Stir in brown sugar and oats. Place about 2 tablespoons crumb topping on each muffin half.

Breakfast Cookies

1 Butter Flavor* CRISCO® Stick or 1 cup Butter Flavor
    CRISCO® all-vegetable shortening
1 cup crunchy peanut butter
3/4 cup granulated sugar
3/4 cup firmly packed brown sugar
2 eggs, beaten
1 1/2 cups all-purpose flour
1 teaspoon baking powder
1 teaspoon baking soda
1 teaspoon ground cinnamon
1 3/4 cups uncooked quick oats
1 1/4 cups raisins
1 medium Granny Smith apple, finely grated, including juice
1/3 cup finely grated carrot
1/4 cup flake coconut (optional)

Butter Flavor Crisco is artificially flavored.

1. Heat oven to 350°F. Place sheets of foil on countertop for cooling cookies. Combine shortening, peanut butter and sugars in large bowl. Beat at medium speed with electric mixer until blended. Beat in eggs.

2. Combine flour, baking powder, baking soda and cinnamon. Add gradually to creamed mixture at low speed. Beat until blended. Stir in oats, raisins, apple, carrot and coconut. Drop by measuring tablespoonfuls onto *ungreased* baking sheet.

3. Bake for 9 to 11 minutes or until just brown around edges. *Do not overbake.* Cool 2 minutes on baking sheet. Remove cookies to foil to cool completely.   *Makes 5 to 6 dozen cookies*

Pecan Country Coffee Cake

$^1/_2$ cup KARO® Light or Dark Corn Syrup, divided

2 tablespoons margarine or butter, softened

2 tablespoons packed brown sugar

1 cup coarsely chopped pecans

1$^1/_2$ cups baking mix

$^1/_3$ cup sugar

$^1/_2$ teaspoon cinnamon

$^1/_3$ cup milk

1 egg

1 teaspoon vanilla

1. Preheat oven to 350°F.

2. In 8-inch square baking pan combine $^1/_4$ cup corn syrup, the margarine and brown sugar. Sprinkle with pecans. Spread mixture evenly over bottom of pan.

3. In medium bowl combine baking mix, sugar and cinnamon. Stir in remaining $^1/_4$ cup corn syrup, the milk, egg and vanilla until well mixed. Pour into pan.

4. Bake 30 minutes or until toothpick inserted into center comes out clean. Loosen edges with knife. Immediately invert onto serving plate. Serve warm.   *Makes 8 servings*

Prep Time: 20 minutes
Bake Time: 30 minutes

Pecan Country Coffee Cake

Gingerbread Streusel Raisin Muffins

1 cup raisins

$^1/_2$ cup boiling water

$^1/_3$ cup margarine or butter, softened

$^3/_4$ cup GRANDMA'S® Molasses (Unsulphured)

1 egg

2 cups all-purpose flour

$1^1/_2$ teaspoons baking soda

$^1/_2$ teaspoon salt

1 teaspoon cinnamon

1 teaspoon ginger

TOPPING

$^1/_3$ cup all-purpose flour

$^1/_4$ cup firmly packed brown sugar

$^1/_4$ cup chopped nuts

3 tablespoons margarine or butter

1 teaspoon cinnamon

Preheat oven to 375°F. Grease bottoms only of 12 muffin cups or line with paper baking cups. In small bowl, cover raisins with boiling water; let stand 5 minutes. In large bowl, beat $^1/_3$ cup margarine and molasses until fluffy. Add egg; beat well. Stir in 2 cups flour, baking soda, salt, 1 teaspoon cinnamon and ginger. Blend just until dry ingredients are moistened. Gently stir in raisins and water. Fill prepared muffin cups $^3/_4$ full. For topping, combine all ingredients in small bowl. Sprinkle over muffins. Bake 20 to 25 minutes or until toothpick inserted in centers comes out clean. Cool 5 minutes; remove from pan. Serve warm.

Makes 12 muffins

Gingerbread Streusel Raisin Muffins

Get Up & Go

Sometimes there's just not enough time in the morning for all you've got to do. But that doesn't mean you have to skip breakfast. These easy-to-prepare morning meals are perfect for when you're running low on time, but you don't want to run low on energy!

Brunch Sandwiches

4 English muffins, split, lightly toasted
8 thin slices CURE 81® ham
8 teaspoons Dijon mustard
8 large eggs, fried or poached
8 slices SARGENTO® Deli Style Sliced Swiss Cheese

1. Top each muffin half with a slice of ham, folding to fit. Spread mustard lightly over ham; top with an egg and one slice cheese.

2. Transfer to foil-lined baking sheet. Broil 4 to 5 inches from heat source until cheese is melted and sandwiches are hot, 2 to 3 minutes.

Makes 4 servings

Preparation Time: 5 minutes
Cooking Time: 10 minutes

Pita in the Morning

1 teaspoon butter or margarine

2 eggs, lightly beaten

$1/4$ teaspoon salt

Dash black pepper

1 whole wheat pita bread, cut in half

$1/4$ cup alfalfa sprouts

2 tablespoons shredded Cheddar cheese

2 tablespoons chopped tomato

Avocado slices (optional)

1. Melt butter at HIGH 30 seconds in microwavable 1-quart casserole.

2. Season eggs with salt and pepper. Add eggs to casserole. Microwave at HIGH $1^{1}/_{2}$ to $2^{1}/_{2}$ minutes, stirring once. Do not overcook; eggs should be soft with no liquid remaining.

3. Open pita to make pockets. Arrange sprouts in pockets. Divide cheese and eggs evenly between pockets. Top with tomato and avocado slices.

Makes 1 sandwich

*For the quickest preparation of this tasty breakfast
sandwich, use packaged shredded cheese and
substitute prepared salsa for the chopped tomato.*

Pita in the Morning

Breakfast in a Cup

    3 cups cooked rice
    1 cup (4 ounces) shredded Cheddar cheese, divided
    1 can (4 ounces) diced green chiles
    1 jar (2 ounces) diced pimientos, drained
  $1/3$ cup skim milk
    2 eggs, beaten
  $1/2$ teaspoon ground cumin
  $1/2$ teaspoon salt
  $1/2$ teaspoon ground black pepper
    Vegetable cooking spray

Combine rice, $1/2$ cup cheese, chiles, pimientos, milk, eggs, cumin, salt and pepper in large bowl. Evenly divide mixture into 12 muffin cups coated with cooking spray. Sprinkle with remaining $1/2$ cup cheese. Bake at 400°F. for 15 minutes or until set. *Makes 12 servings*

Tip: Breakfast Cups may be stored in the freezer in a freezer bag or tightly sealed container. To reheat frozen Breakfast Cups, microwave each cup on HIGH 1 minute.

Favorite recipe from **USA Rice Federation**

Nutty Apricot Warm-Up

3¼ cups milk

¼ teaspoon ground cinnamon

½ cup CREAM OF WHEAT® Cereal (1-minute, 2½-minute or
10-minute stovetop cooking)

1 (17-ounce) can apricot halves, drained and chopped

⅓ cup seedless raisins

⅓ cup PLANTERS® Pecans, coarsely chopped

Brown sugar, optional

1. Bring milk and cinnamon to a boil in large saucepan over medium-high heat. Slowly sprinkle in cereal, stirring constantly 2 to 3 minutes or until mixture thickens.

2. Stir in apricots, raisins and pecans; reduce heat to low. Cook and stir 5 minutes more. Serve topped with brown sugar and additional milk, if desired.

Makes 6 servings

Microwave Directions: Mix milk, cinnamon and cereal in 2-quart microwavable bowl. Microwave, uncovered, at HIGH (100%) 8 to 10 minutes or until slightly thickened, stirring after 4 minutes. Stir in apricots, raisins and pecans. Microwave 3 to 4 minutes or until desired consistency. Let stand 2 minutes before serving.

Cinnamon Fruit Crunch

1 cup low-fat granola cereal

¹/₄ cup toasted sliced almonds

1 tablespoon reduced-calorie margarine

2 tablespoons plus 1 teaspoon packed brown sugar, divided

2¹/₄ teaspoons ground cinnamon, divided

¹/₂ cup vanilla nonfat yogurt

¹/₈ teaspoon ground nutmeg

2 cans (16 ounces each) mixed fruit chunks in juice, drained

Combine granola and almonds in small bowl. Melt margarine in small saucepan. Blend in 2 tablespoons brown sugar and 2 teaspoons cinnamon; simmer until sugar dissolves, about 2 minutes. Toss with granola and almonds; cool. Combine yogurt, 1 teaspoon brown sugar, ¹/₄ teaspoon cinnamon and nutmeg in small bowl. To serve, spoon approximately ¹/₂ cup chunky mixed fruit onto each serving plate. Top with yogurt mixture and sprinkle with granola mixture. *Makes 6 servings*

Cinnamon Fruit Crunch

Maple Apple Oatmeal

2 cups apple juice

1 1/2 cups water

1/3 cup AUNT JEMIMA® Syrup

1/2 teaspoon ground cinnamon

1/4 teaspoon salt (optional)

2 cups QUAKER® Oats (quick or old fashioned, uncooked)

1 cup chopped fresh unpeeled apple (about 1 medium)

In a 3-quart saucepan, bring juice, water, syrup, cinnamon and salt to a boil. Stir in oats and apple. Return to a boil; reduce heat to medium-low. Cook about 1 minute for quick oats (or 5 minutes for old fashioned oats) or until most of liquid is absorbed, stirring occasionally. Let stand until of desired consistency.   *Makes 4 servings*

*Place the chopped apple in a bowl of water mixed
with a little lemon juice so that it won't turn brown
while you're waiting for the juice mixture to boil.*

Breakfast Risotto

4 cups cooked brown rice

2 cups (8 ounces) shredded GJETOST Cheese

1 cup 1% low fat milk

$^{1}/_{2}$ cup chopped walnuts or pecans (optional)

$^{1}/_{2}$ cup raisins

Scant teaspoon cinnamon

In saucepan over medium heat, gently stir all ingredients together until hot and cheese is melted. Or, stir ingredients in microwave-safe pie plate and microwave on HIGH (100% power) $2^{1}/_{2}$ minutes. Stir, then cook 1 additional minute if necessary.

Serve with green and red apple slices, strawberries or other fruit.

Makes 6 to 8 servings

Ham Scramble

1/4 cup butter or margarine

2 cups (12 ounces) chopped CURE 81® ham

2 tablespoons sliced green onion

8 eggs, beaten

1/2 cup sour cream

2 tablespoons grated Parmesan cheese

1/2 teaspoon salt

1/4 teaspoon black pepper

3 English muffins, split, toasted and buttered

In large skillet melt butter. Add ham and green onion. Cook over medium-high heat, stirring constantly until onion is tender. In bowl, beat together eggs, sour cream, Parmesan cheese, salt and black pepper. Add to ham mixture. Cook, without stirring, until mixture begins to set on bottom. Draw a spatula across bottom of pan to form large curds. Continue cooking until eggs are thickened but still moist; do not stir constantly. Serve immediately over toasted English muffin halves.

Makes 6 servings

Ham Scramble

Breakfast Nachos

1 ³/₄ cups (1-pound can) ORTEGA® Refried Beans, heated

4 cups (4 ounces) tortilla chips

4 eggs, scrambled

1 ¹/₂ cups (6 ounces) shredded Cheddar or Monterey Jack cheese

¹/₄ cup ORTEGA® Sliced Jalapeños

ORTEGA® Thick & Chunky Salsa, hot, medium or mild

Sour cream

Additional topping suggestions: guacamole, chopped green onions, chopped fresh cilantro, sliced ripe olives

SPREAD beans onto bottom of large ovenproof platter or jelly-roll pan. Arrange chips over beans. Top with eggs, cheese and jalapeños.

PLACE under preheated broiler, 4 inches away from heat source, for 1 to 1 ¹/₂ minutes or until cheese is melted. Top with salsa, sour cream and additional toppings.   *Makes 4 to 6 servings*

Breakfast Nachos

Breakfast S'mores

¹/₂ package KAVLI® Muesli crispbreads, cut in half crosswise while
 still wrapped
1 apple, thinly sliced
1 nectarine, thinly sliced
1 banana, thinly sliced
¹/₄ cup natural-style peanut butter, with oil poured off
1 tablespoon honey
1 cup mini marshmallows

Arrange 9 crispbread pieces on baking sheet. (Reserve remaining 9 pieces for tops.)

Place sliced fruit on crispbreads in thin layers* (about ¹/₂ inch high).

Mix peanut butter with honey and place ¹/₄ teaspoon on center of each fruit layer, circling it with 2 to 3 mini marshmallows.

Bake in a 350°F oven 4 to 8 minutes or until marshmallows are melted. Place Kavli® lids on top and serve.   *Makes 9 s'mores*

Tip: Keep fruits separate for kids' s'mores; mix fruits for teens and adults.

Fat-Free Tropical Shake

1 cup EGG BEATERS® Healthy Real Egg Product
1 cup cold skim milk
1 small banana, cut into chunks
1 small mango,* peeled and cut into chunks (about 1 cup)

One cup guava, papaya or pineapple chunks may be substituted.

In electric blender container, blend Egg Beaters, milk, banana and mango for 1 minute or until smooth. Serve immediately.

Makes 4 (8-ounce) servings

Prep Time: 5 minutes

Note: Refrigerate unused portion. Must be used within 48 hours.

Nectarine Whirl

1 Chilean nectarine or peach, cut into chunks
$^{1}/_{2}$ cup 1% milk
$^{1}/_{2}$ cup orange juice
1 tablespoon honey
$^{1}/_{4}$ teaspoon almond extract
2 ice cubes, cracked

Place all ingredients in blender. Blend at high speed 15 seconds or until smooth. Serve immediately.

Makes 1$^{1}/_{2}$ cups (1 serving)

Favorite recipe from **Chilean Fresh Fruit Association**

Baked Eggs

4 eggs

4 teaspoons milk

    Salt and black pepper to taste

1. Preheat oven to 375°F. Grease 4 small baking dishes or custard cups.

2. Break 1 egg into each dish. Add 1 teaspoon milk to each dish. Season with salt and pepper.

3. Bake about 15 minutes or until set.   *Makes 4 servings*

For added flavor and color, before baking, top the eggs with 1 tablespoon shredded cheese, salsa or chopped ham, or 1 teaspoon minced fresh herbs. Then simply bake as directed.

Baked Eggs

Greek Isles Omelet

Nonstick cooking spray
1/4 cup chopped onion
1/4 cup canned artichoke hearts, rinsed and drained
1/4 cup washed and torn spinach leaves
1/4 cup chopped plum tomato
1 cup cholesterol-free egg substitute
2 tablespoons sliced pitted ripe olives, rinsed and drained
Dash black pepper

1. Spray small nonstick skillet with cooking spray; heat over medium heat until hot. Cook and stir onion 2 minutes or until crisp-tender.

2. Add artichoke hearts. Cook and stir until heated through. Add spinach and tomato; toss briefly. Remove from heat. Transfer vegetables to small bowl. Wipe out skillet and spray with cooking spray.

3. Combine egg substitute, olives and pepper in medium bowl. Heat skillet over medium heat until hot. Pour egg mixture into skillet. Cook over medium heat 5 to 7 minutes; as eggs begin to set, gently lift edges of omelet with spatula and tilt skillet so that uncooked portion flows underneath.

4. When egg mixture is set, spoon vegetable mixture over half of omelet. Loosen omelet with spatula and fold in half. Slide omelet onto serving plate. *Makes 2 servings*

Greek Isles Omelet

Company's Coming

Dazzle your guests with an outstanding array of mouthwatering breakfast and brunch temptations. With the many delicious choices here, you're sure to please everyone!

Egg and Sausage Breakfast Strudel

1 pound BOB EVANS® Original Recipe Roll Sausage

3/4 cup finely grated Parmesan cheese

1 (10³/4-ounce) can condensed cream of mushroom soup

2 hard-cooked eggs, cut into 1/4-inch cubes

1/2 cup thinly sliced green onions

1/4 cup chopped fresh parsley

1 (16-ounce) package frozen phyllo dough, thawed according to package directions

Butter-flavored nonstick cooking spray *or* 1/2 cup melted butter or margarine

Crumble and cook sausage in medium skillet until browned. Drain off any drippings; place sausage in medium bowl. Add cheese, soup, eggs, green onions and parsley; stir gently until blended. Cover and chill at least 4 hours.

Preheat oven to 375°F. Layer 4 sheets of phyllo dough, coating each sheet with cooking spray or brushing with melted butter before stacking. Cut stack in half lengthwise. Shape 1/3 cup filling into log and place at bottom end of 1 stack. Fold in sides to cover filling; roll up phyllo dough and filling jelly roll style. Seal edges and spray roll with cooking spray or brush with butter. Repeat with remaining phyllo dough and filling. Place rolls on ungreased baking sheet, seam sides down. Bake 15 to 20 minutes or until golden brown. Serve hot. Refrigerate leftovers.

Makes 10 strudels

Note: Unbaked strudels can be wrapped and refrigerated up to 24 hours, or frozen up to 1 month. If frozen, allow additional baking time.

Tropical Chicken Salad

Tropical Salad Dressing (recipe follows)
3 cups cubed cooked chicken
$3/4$ cup coarsely chopped celery
$3/4$ cup seedless red or green grape halves
$3/4$ cup coarsely chopped macadamia nuts or toasted almonds
Lettuce leaves
Strawberries and kiwifruit for garnish
Toasted flaked coconut for garnish*

To toast coconut, spread evenly on cookie sheet. Toast in preheated 350°F oven 7 minutes. Stir and toast 1 to 2 minutes more or until light golden brown.

Prepare Tropical Salad Dressing. Combine chicken, celery, grapes and nuts in large bowl; stir in 1 cup dressing. Cover; refrigerate 1 hour. Mound chicken salad on lettuce-lined platter or individual plates. Garnish with strawberries, kiwifruit and coconut. Serve with remaining dressing.

Makes 4 servings

Tropical Salad Dressing: Place $1/2$ cup cream of coconut, $1/3$ cup red wine vinegar, 1 teaspoon dry mustard, 1 teaspoon salt and 1 clove garlic, peeled, in blender or food processor container. With processor on, slowly add 1 cup vegetable oil in thin stream, processing until smooth.

Tropical Chicken Salad

Stuffed French Toast with Apricot and Orange Marmalade Sauce

Apricot and Orange Marmalade Sauce (page 100)
1 package (8 ounces) cream cheese, softened
1/2 cup (4 ounces) part-skim ricotta cheese
1/4 cup orange marmalade
2 tablespoons sugar
1 loaf (16 ounces) Vienna bread
4 eggs
1 cup milk
1 teaspoon vanilla
Grated nutmeg

1. Prepare Apricot and Orange Marmalade Sauce. Preheat oven to 475°F. Lightly grease baking sheet.

2. Beat cream cheese in medium bowl with electric mixer at medium speed until smooth. Beat in ricotta, marmalade and sugar.

3. Trim ends from bread; discard. Slice bread into 8 (1 1/2-inch-thick) slices. Cut pocket in each bread slice by cutting through top crust and almost to bottom, leaving sides of bread slices intact. Carefully fill each pocket with about 3 tablespoons cream cheese mixture.

4. Beat eggs in large shallow dish. Add milk and vanilla; whisk until blended. Dip 1 filled bread slice at a time into egg mixture; turn over and allow to soak up egg mixture.

continued on page 100

Stuffed French Toast with Apricot and Orange Marmalade Sauce

Stuffed French Toast with Apricot and Orange Marmalade Sauce, continued

5. Place filled slices onto prepared baking sheet. Sprinkle with nutmeg. Bake 5 minutes or until golden on bottom. Turn slices over with spatula; sprinkle with nutmeg. Bake 3 to 5 minutes or until golden on bottom. Baked toast should feel just slightly crisp on surface. Serve with Apricot and Orange Marmalade Sauce. Garnish, if desired.

Makes 6 to 8 servings

Apricot and Orange Marmalade Sauce

> 1 tablespoon butter or margarine
> 1 1/2 cups chopped peeled fresh apricots or peaches
> 1 cup orange marmalade
> 1/2 teaspoon ground nutmeg

1. Melt butter in medium saucepan over medium-high heat. Add apricots; cook and stir 5 to 10 minutes or until fork-tender.

2. Add marmalade and nutmeg; stir until marmalade is melted. Transfer mixture to food processor; process until apricots are finely chopped. Serve warm.

Makes about 2 cups

5 to 7 whole fresh apricots or 2 to 3 medium peaches will yield about 1 1/2 cups chopped fruit.

Black Bean Turkey Pepper Salad

$3/4$ pound fully cooked honey-roasted turkey breast, cut into $1/4$-inch cubes

1 small red bell pepper, cut into $1/4$-inch cubes

1 small yellow bell pepper, cut into $1/4$-inch cubes

1 can (15 ounces) black beans, rinsed and drained

1 cup thinly sliced green onions

$3/4$ cup chopped fresh cilantro

2 tablespoons olive oil

1 tablespoon red wine vinegar

1 teaspoon ground cumin

$1/4$ teaspoon cayenne pepper

1. In large bowl combine turkey, red and yellow peppers, black beans, onions and cilantro.

2. In small bowl whisk together oil, vinegar, cumin and cayenne pepper. Fold dressing into turkey mixture. Cover and refrigerate 1 hour.

Makes 6 servings

Favorite recipe from **National Turkey Federation**

Cheddar Pepper Muffins

2 cups all-purpose flour

1 tablespoon sugar

1 tablespoon baking powder

1 teaspoon black pepper

$^1/_2$ teaspoon salt

$1^1/_4$ cups milk

$^1/_4$ cup vegetable oil

1 egg

1 cup (4 ounces) shredded sharp Cheddar cheese, divided

Preheat oven to 400°F. Generously grease or paper-line 12 ($2^1/_2$-inch) muffin cups. Combine flour, sugar, baking powder, pepper and salt in large bowl. Combine milk, oil and egg in small bowl until blended. Stir into flour mixture just until moistened. Fold in $^3/_4$ cup cheese. Spoon into muffin cups. Sprinkle with remaining cheese. Bake 15 to 20 minutes or until light golden brown. Cool in pan on wire rack 5 minutes. Remove from pan; serve warm.   *Makes 12 muffins*

Cheddar Pepper Muffins

Shrimp Louis Muffins

1 cup HELLMANN'S® or BEST FOODS® Real, Light or Low
  Fat Mayonnaise Dressing

$1/2$ cup chili sauce

1 teaspoon lemon juice

1 teaspoon prepared horseradish

$1/2$ teaspoon grated onion

$1/8$ teaspoon salt

$1/8$ teaspoon freshly ground pepper

4 Thomas' original flavor English muffins, split, toasted and
  buttered

Lettuce leaves

4 hard-cooked eggs, sliced

$3/4$ pound medium shrimp, shelled, deveined and cooked

1. In small bowl, stir mayonnaise, chili sauce, lemon juice, horseradish, onion, salt and pepper until blended. Cover; chill.

2. Top each muffin half with lettuce, egg slices, shrimp and dressing.

Makes 4 servings

Shrimp Louis Muffins

Cardamom-Spiked Fresh Lemonade Spritzer

40 whole white cardamom pods, cracked
1 1/4 cups sugar
3 cups water
2 cups fresh lemon juice
1 bottle (750 ml) Asti Spumante or club soda
Additional sugar (optional)
Ice
Mint leaves for garnish

Combine cardamom pods with 1 1/4 cups sugar and water in medium saucepan. Cook and stir over high heat until mixture comes to a boil and sugar dissolves. Reduce heat to low; cover and simmer 30 minutes. Remove from heat; cool completely. Refrigerate 2 hours or up to 3 days.

Pour mixture through strainer into 3-quart pitcher; discard pods. Stir in lemon juice and Asti Spumante. Stir in additional sugar to taste. Serve over ice. Garnish, if desired. *Makes 6 servings*

Breakfast Bread Pudding with Berry Sauce

8 slices cinnamon raisin bread, cubed

2 cups skim milk

1 cup EGG BEATERS® Healthy Real Egg Product

1/4 cup sugar

1 teaspoon vanilla extract

1/2 teaspoon ground nutmeg

1/2 cup maple-flavored syrup

2 tablespoons FLEISCHMANN'S® Original Margarine

1 cup sliced strawberries

1/2 cup blueberries

1 teaspoon lemon juice

1 teaspoon lemon peel

Evenly divide bread cubes among 8 greased heatproof (6-ounce) custard cups or ramekins. In medium bowl, combine milk, Egg Beaters®, sugar, vanilla and nutmeg. Evenly pour mixture over bread cubes. Place cups in roasting pan filled with 1-inch depth hot water. Bake at 325°F for 35 to 45 minutes or until set. Let stand for 5 minutes.

In small saucepan, heat syrup and margarine until blended. Stir in fruit, lemon juice and peel; heat through. Unmold puddings onto individual serving plates; serve with berry sauce.   *Makes 8 servings*

Prep Time: 15 minutes
Cook Time: 45 minutes

Elegant Crabmeat Frittata

3 tablespoons butter or margarine, divided
$1/4$ pound fresh mushrooms, sliced
2 green onions, cut into thin slices
8 eggs, separated
$1/4$ cup milk
$1/4$ teaspoon salt
$1/2$ teaspoon hot pepper sauce
$1/2$ pound lump crabmeat or imitation crabmeat, flaked and picked
    over to remove any shells
$1/2$ cup (2 ounces) shredded Swiss cheese

1. Melt 2 tablespoons butter in large ovenproof skillet over medium-high heat. Add mushrooms and onions; cook and stir 3 to 5 minutes or until vegetables are tender. Remove from skillet; set aside.

2. Beat egg yolks with electric mixer at high speed until slightly thickened and lemon color. Stir in milk, salt and hot pepper sauce.

3. Beat egg whites in clean large bowl with electric mixer at high speed until foamy. Gradually add to egg yolk mixture, whisking just until blended.

4. Melt remaining 1 tablespoon butter in skillet. Pour egg mixture into skillet. Cook until eggs are almost set. Remove from heat.

5. Preheat broiler. Broil frittata 4 to 6 inches from heat until top is set. Top with crabmeat, mushroom mixture and cheese. Return frittata to broiler; broil until cheese is melted. Garnish, if desired. Serve immediately.

Makes 4 servings

Elegant Crabmeat Frittata

Festive Caramel Floral Rolls

2 cups water

1 cup firmly packed dark brown sugar, divided

$^{1}/_{2}$ cup shortening

$5^{1}/_{2}$ to 6 cups all-purpose flour, divided

2 packages active dry yeast

2 teaspoons salt

2 teaspoons baking powder

2 teaspoons vanilla

3 tablespoons butter

3 tablespoons milk

1. Heat water, $^{1}/_{2}$ cup brown sugar and shortening in small saucepan over medium heat until sugar is dissolved and shortening is melted. Remove from heat; cool to 120° to 130°F.

2. Combine 3 cups flour, yeast, salt and baking powder in large bowl. Add sugar mixture and vanilla; beat vigorously 2 minutes. Add remaining flour, $^{1}/_{4}$ cup at a time, until dough begins to pull away from side of bowl. Turn out dough onto floured work surface; flatten slightly. Knead 10 minutes or until smooth and elastic, adding flour if necessary to prevent sticking.

3. Shape dough into ball. Place in large lightly oiled bowl; turn dough over once to oil surface. Cover with towel; let rise in warm place about 1 hour or until doubled in bulk.

4. Turn dough out onto lightly oiled work surface. Divide into 24 equal pieces. Form each piece into ball. Cover with towel on work surface; let rest 5 minutes.

continued on page 112

Festive Caramel Floral Rolls

Festive Caramel Floral Rolls, continued

5. Preheat oven to 375°F. Lightly grease 2 baking sheets. Roll 12 balls of dough into 10-inch ropes. Keep remaining balls covered. Tie one 10-inch rope into knot. Place in center of prepared baking sheet. Form remaining 11 ropes into tear drop shapes so loose ends touch. Place on baking sheet around dough knot to form daisy-like flower. Repeat with remaining dough.

6. Bake 25 minutes or until deep golden brown.

7. While bread is baking, melt butter in small saucepan over medium-low heat. When butter begins to bubble, add remaining $1/2$ cup brown sugar; stir 3 minutes. Add milk. Bring to a boil without stirring. Cook 3 minutes; remove from heat and cool.

8. When bread is done baking, immediately remove bread from baking sheet and cool on wire rack. Brush each loaf with butter mixture.

Makes 2 loaves

This bread makes a great housewarming or holiday gift. Simply wrap it in colored plastic wrap or cellophane, then tie the wrap closed with festive curling ribbons.

Pasta with White Beans and Mushrooms

2 tablespoons vegetable oil

1 pound fresh white mushrooms, halved or quartered

1 cup chopped onions

1 cup diced carrots

1 teaspoon minced garlic

1 can (19 ounces) white kidney beans, rinsed and drained

1 can (13¾ ounces) ready-to-serve chicken broth

8 ounces smoked ham, diced

1 teaspoon Italian seasoning

4 cups (8 ounces) uncooked wagon wheel pasta

1 cup diced tomato

Salt and pepper (optional)

Grated Parmesan cheese (optional)

Chopped fresh parsley (optional)

Heat oil in heavy saucepan until hot. Add mushrooms, onions, carrots and garlic; cook, stirring frequently, 6 to 8 minutes or until vegetables are tender. Add beans, chicken broth, ham and Italian seasoning; bring to a boil. Reduce heat and simmer, covered, about 20 minutes.

Meanwhile, cook pasta according to package directions; drain. Transfer to large serving bowl. Stir tomato into saucepan; cook about 2 minutes or until heated through. Season with salt and pepper to taste, if desired. Spoon over pasta. Sprinkle with grated Parmesan cheese and fresh parsley, if desired.   *Makes 4 servings*

Favorite recipe from **Mushroom Council**

Mocha Supreme

    2 quarts brewed strong coffee
$^1/_2$ cup instant hot chocolate beverage mix
    1 cinnamon stick, broken into halves
    1 cup whipping cream
    1 tablespoon powdered sugar

Slow Cooker Directions

Place coffee, hot chocolate mix and cinnamon stick halves in slow cooker; stir. Cover and cook on HIGH 2 to $2^1/_2$ hours or until hot. Remove and discard cinnamon stick halves.

Beat cream in medium bowl with electric mixer on high speed until soft peaks form. Add powdered sugar; beat until stiff peaks form. Ladle hot beverage into mugs; top with whipped cream.   *Makes 8 servings*

Mocha Supreme

Southwest Sausage Bread

    1 cup water
    1 package active dry yeast
    1 tablespoon sugar
 $1^{3}/_{4}$ to $2^{1}/_{4}$ cups all-purpose flour, divided
 $1^{1}/_{2}$ cups whole wheat flour, divided
    1 egg
    2 tablespoons vegetable oil
 $^{1}/_{4}$ teaspoon salt
    1 medium onion, finely chopped
    4 ounces dry chorizo or pepperoni sausage, chopped
    1 cup (4 ounces) shredded Monterey Jack cheese

Heat water in saucepan over low heat until water reaches 105° to 110°F.
Sprinkle yeast and sugar over heated water in large bowl; stir until
dissolved. Let stand 5 minutes or until bubbly. Add 1 cup all-purpose
flour, 1 cup whole wheat flour, egg, oil and salt. Beat until blended. Beat at
medium speed 3 minutes. Stir in remaining $^{1}/_{2}$ cup whole-wheat flour and
enough all-purpose flour, about $^{3}/_{4}$ cup, to make soft dough.

Turn out dough onto all-purpose floured surface; flatten. Knead 5 to
8 minutes or until smooth and elastic; gradually add remaining $^{1}/_{2}$ cup
all-purpose flour to prevent sticking, if necessary. Shape into ball; place in
lightly greased bowl. Turn dough over. Cover; let rise in warm place 1 hour
or until doubled. Cook onion and sausage in skillet over medium heat
5 minutes or until onion is tender. Drain on paper towels.

Punch down dough. Knead on floured surface 1 minute. Cover; let rest
10 minutes.

continued on page 118

Southwest Sausage Bread

Southwest Sausage Bread, continued

Spray 9×5-inch loaf pan with nonstick cooking spray. Roll dough into 24×11-inch rectangle. Sprinkle sausage mixture and cheese over dough. Roll up dough jelly-roll style from short end. Pinch seam and ends to seal. Cut dough lengthwise into halves. With cut sides facing up, twist halves together. Pinch ends to seal. Place in pan, cut sides up. Let rise 1 hour or until doubled.

Preheat oven to 375°F. Bake 30 minutes or until loaf sounds hollow when tapped. Remove from pan; let cool.   *Makes 12 servings*

Turkey Fruited Bow Tie Salad

    1/2 pound no-salt turkey breast, cut into 1/2-inch cubes
    2 cups bow tie pasta, cooked according to package directions and
        drained
    1 can (10 1/2 ounces) mandarin oranges, drained
    1 medium red apple, chopped
    1 cup seedless grapes, cut in half
    1/2 cup celery, sliced
    1/2 cup low-fat lemon yogurt
    2 tablespoons frozen orange juice concentrate, thawed
    1/4 teaspoon ground ginger

1. In large bowl, combine turkey, pasta, oranges, apple, grapes and celery.

2. In small bowl, combine yogurt, juice concentrate and ginger. Fold dressing into turkey mixture and toss to coat. Cover and refrigerate until ready to serve.   *Makes 4 servings*

Favorite recipe from **National Turkey Federation**

Vegetable Soufflé in Pepper Cups

1 cup chopped broccoli

¹/₂ cup shredded carrot

¹/₄ cup chopped onion

1 teaspoon dried basil leaves, crushed

¹/₂ teaspoon ground black pepper

2 teaspoons FLEISCHMANN'S® Original Margarine

2 tablespoons all-purpose flour

1 cup skim milk

1 cup EGG BEATERS® Healthy Real Egg Product

3 large red, green or yellow bell peppers, halved lengthwise

In nonstick skillet over medium-high heat, cook and stir broccoli, carrot, onion, basil and black pepper in margarine until vegetables are tender. Stir in flour until smooth. Gradually add milk, stirring constantly until thickened. Remove from heat; set aside.

In medium bowl, with electric mixer at high speed, beat Egg Beaters® until foamy, about 3 minutes. Gently fold into broccoli mixture; spoon into bell pepper halves. Place in 13×9-inch baking pan. Bake at 375°F for 30 to 35 minutes or until knife inserted in centers comes out clean. Garnish as desired and serve immediately. *Makes 6 servings*

Ham-Broccoli Quiche

1 cup sliced fresh mushrooms

1 clove garlic, minced

2 teaspoons butter or margarine

$^1/_2$ cup shredded Swiss cheese

1 (9-inch) pastry shell

1$^1/_2$ cups (8 ounces) chopped CURE 81® ham

1 cup cooked, chopped broccoli

3 eggs

1 cup milk

2 teaspoons all-purpose flour

$^1/_4$ teaspoon white pepper

Dash ground nutmeg

2 tablespoons grated Romano or Parmesan cheese

Heat oven to 350°F. In skillet over medium-high heat, sauté mushrooms and garlic in butter until tender. Sprinkle Swiss cheese in pastry shell. Top with mushroom mixture, ham and broccoli. In bowl, beat together eggs, milk, flour, white pepper and nutmeg; pour into pastry shell. Sprinkle with Romano or Parmesan cheese. Bake 35 to 40 minutes or until knife inserted near center comes out clean. Let stand 10 minutes before serving.

Makes 6 servings

Ham-Broccoli Quiche

ACKNOWLEDGMENTS

The publisher would like to thank the companies and organizations listed below for the use of their recipes and photographs in this publication.

Bays English Muffin Corporation

Bestfoods

Bob Evans®

Cherry Marketing Institute

Chilean Fresh Fruit Association

Colorado Potato Administrative Committee·

ConAgra Grocery Products Company

Cream of Wheat® Cereal

DAVIS® Baking Powder

Egg Beaters®

Grandma's® is a registered trademark of Mott's, Inc.

Hebrew National®

Hormel Foods Corporation

The HV Company

Kraft Foods, Inc.

Mushroom Council

National Turkey Federation

Nestlé USA, Inc.

Norseland, Inc.

PLANTERS® Nuts

The Procter & Gamble Company

The Quaker® Oatmeal Kitchens

Reckitt Benckiser

Sargento® Foods Inc.

The J.M. Smucker Company

The Sugar Association, Inc.

USA Rice Federation

Washington Apple Commission

Wisconsin Milk Marketing Board

INDEX

VOLUME MEASUREMENTS (dry)

$1/8$ teaspoon = 0.5 mL
$1/4$ teaspoon = 1 mL
$1/2$ teaspoon = 2 mL
$3/4$ teaspoon = 4 mL
1 teaspoon = 5 mL
1 tablespoon = 15 mL
2 tablespoons = 30 mL
$1/4$ cup = 60 mL
$1/3$ cup = 75 mL
$1/2$ cup = 125 mL
$2/3$ cup = 150 mL
$3/4$ cup = 175 mL
1 cup = 250 mL
2 cups = 1 pint = 500 mL
3 cups = 750 mL
4 cups = 1 quart = 1 L

VOLUME MEASUREMENTS (fluid)

1 fluid ounce (2 tablespoons) = 30 mL
4 fluid ounces ($1/2$ cup) = 125 mL
8 fluid ounces (1 cup) = 250 mL
12 fluid ounces ($1 1/2$ cups) = 375 mL
16 fluid ounces (2 cups) = 500 mL

WEIGHTS (mass)

$1/2$ ounce = 15 g
1 ounce = 30 g
3 ounces = 90 g
4 ounces = 120 g
8 ounces = 225 g
10 ounces = 285 g
12 ounces = 360 g
16 ounces = 1 pound = 450 g

DIMENSIONS

$1/16$ inch = 2 mm
$1/8$ inch = 3 mm
$1/4$ inch = 6 mm
$1/2$ inch = 1.5 cm
$3/4$ inch = 2 cm
1 inch = 2.5 cm

OVEN TEMPERATURES

250°F = 120°C
275°F = 140°C
300°F = 150°C
325°F = 160°C
350°F = 180°C
375°F = 190°C
400°F = 200°C
425°F = 220°C
450°F = 230°C

BAKING PAN SIZES

Utensil	Size in Inches/Quarts	Metric Volume	Size in Centimeters
Baking or Cake Pan (square or rectangular)	8×8×2	2 L	20×20×5
	9×9×2	2.5 L	23×23×5
	12×8×2	3 L	30×20×5
	13×9×2	3.5 L	33×23×5
Loaf Pan	8×4×3	1.5 L	20×10×7
	9×5×3	2 L	23×13×7
Round Layer Cake Pan	8×1½	1.2 L	20×4
	9×1½	1.5 L	23×4
Pie Plate	8×1¼	750 mL	20×3
	9×1¼	1 L	23×3
Baking Dish or Casserole	1 quart	1 L	—
	1½ quart	1.5 L	—
	2 quart	2 L	—